Next Stop: You

The Journey of SanRul

"Dr Harshita S Jaiman"

"SanRul"

 *Table of Contents — Next stop: You*

Part I: When Hearts First Met

Chapter 1: A Glance That Changed Everything
Chapter 2: Coffee, Chaos & Chemistry
Chapter 3: Conversations On Air
Chapter 4: The Day My World Shifted

Part II: Through the Storm & Love — But Stronger

Part III: The Family Walls
  . Us vs. Them
Part IV: The Break We Didn't Want

- A Chapter Left Unwritten

Part V: Finding My Way Back to Us
  When the Universe Whispered "Try Again"
  Our Ending That Feels Like a New Beginning

Afterword: A Love That Wrote Itself

About the Author

Dedication....

To you—   **"Sandeep..."**

Who Taught Me That Love Isn't Always Spoken,
But Felt in the Stillness Between Words,
In the Gentle Quiet of Shared Moments.
Your Silent Love Became My Greatest Lesson,
A Language Only Our Hearts Could Understand.
Thank You for Showing Me How to Love,
Even When the World Was Silent.

Acknowledgements….

Writing this book has been a journey of the heart, and I could not have done it without the love, support, and inspiration of many wonderful people.

First and foremost, to my partner — my best friend , my greatest adventure. This story is ours, born from the moments we've shared, the storms we've weathered, and the dreams we continue to chase. Thank you for loving me fiercely and honestly, and for being the kind of love worth writing about.

To our families, thank you for supporting us through every chapter. Your faith in us gave us strength when we needed it most.

With gratitude and all my heart,

"Dr Harshita S Jaiman"

Preface....

This isn't just a story — it's a memory stitched with laughter, distance, and the quiet hope that real love always finds its way back.

I didn't write this to be perfect. I wrote it to be true — to capture the moments that shaped us, the silences that spoke, the storms we survived, and the love that stayed.

In these pages live two imperfect souls growing, breaking, healing, and choosing each other again.

This isn't a fairy tale. It's better. It's real.

With love,

"Dr Harshita S Jaiman"

- "Attention passengers"

- - "The train of love is arriving on schedule, a boy will extend his hand to help a girl, and her hand will hold his forever."

- - "Please be informed, the train from Rajgarh will depart shortly, but the journey of love will never end, a boy and a girl will forever be connected."

Part I:

"When We First Met"

Chapter 1:

A Glance That Changed Everything

"SanRul"

The Train Was Late, But The Time Was Right.......

"Late train, but on the right way,

Life's journey unfolds day by day.

Though delayed, still moving ahead,

The path unwinds, where dreams are fed."

....

"Delayed train, but heart's on track,

Start loving life and never look back.

Forever in joy, we'll find our way,

And every moment will brighten the day."

"SanRul"

"A helping hand, a loving deed,

Forever binds, a heart's noble creed.

In times of need, when support's shown,

Love blossoms, forever to be known."

"A hand I held for help one day,

You grasped it tight, forever to stay.

A moment's aid, a lifetime's bond,

Our story began, a love beyond."

"All The Best Instead of Congratulation" ....

....

"Coincidence brought us face to face, job's new phase,
'all the best' in nervous haste."

"Met by chance, job's delight, 'all the best' said tight,
congratulations in sight."

"Nervous meet, job's Congratulations, 'all the best'
instead whispered glory."

"SanRul"

"Train delayed, but heart's still true,

Life's journey unfolds, with moments anew.

We walk together, side by side,

Love's story woven, as life's path divides."

....

"Train was late, but fate was bright,

You met me there, and everything's alright.

In delay's unexpected twist of fate,

We found each other, a love so great."

"SanRul"

"Awaited message, uncertain fate,

Yet hearts held hope, an expectant state.

Message arrived, and words began to flow,

Distance between hearts, now bridged to know."

....

"Message awaited, with hopeful heart,

Uncertainty faded, as words did start.

Connection made, a bond took hold,

Conversation flowed, stories to be told."

"SanRul"

"Words of friendship, heartfelt and true,

Some hurts lingered, but love shone through.

You claimed me yours, with understanding eyes,

A bond formed strong, a love that never dies."

....

"Conversations flowed, like heart's own stream,

Some words hurt, but love's essence beamed.

You saw me yours, with gentle might,

In your words, my heart took flight."

"HarSanHitaDeep"
......Love for life

"A mistake was made, friendship broke apart,

Small reason, but heartache touched the heart.

Couldn't muster courage to say sorry true,

Now memories remain, haunting me anew."

"SanRul"

"Talk resumed, a new meetup born,

What happened, past lessons learned, new start sworn.

No more heartache, like before,

New memories formed, love's path explored."

"SanRul"

"Conversation revived, new chapter unfolds,

Past behind, present moments told.

Fresh beginnings, hearts now align,

Rekindled bond, love's embers shine."

2010 to Now………………

"Once unknown, now discovered true,

Childhood love, now understood anew.

More than I thought, it's grown so deep,

Love's complexity, now I keep."

"SanRul"

Strangers to friends............

"Not unknown, but now truly known,

Heart's depths revealed, love's seeds sown.

What was hidden, now unveiled stands,

Your love recognized, in tender hands."

"SanRul"

"Once strangers, now hearts entwined,

Unknown no more, love's path defined.

In your eyes, a spark I see,

Connection deep, destiny."

"SanRul"

"Not unknown, but now revealed,

Childhood love, in heart concealed.

More than imagined, it's grown so bright,

Love's beauty shines, in morning light."

Wednesday, 14 June 2017

"HarSanHitaDeep"
......Love for life

"SanRul"

"Somehow, love just happened,

An unknown connection, now defined.

Conversations started, hearts aligned,

Now this bond, for lifeetime."

"HarSanHitaDeep"
......Love for life

The Beginning 2015

"Started with a status copy,

Love's journey began, now it's destiny.

Words grew, hearts connected,

Now this love, forever etched."

....

"Status copied, love sparked within,

Unplanned connection, now a win.

Words flowed free, hearts now align,

This bond's story, forever divine."

"SanRul"

"Status posts sparked conversations deep,

Love's flame ignited, hearts now keep.

Unspoken words, now voiced true,

Heartfelt bond, forever new."

....

"Status posts bridged our gap,

Conversations flowed, love's map.

Words from the heart, now freely shared,

Love's path unfolded, together we care."

Love via Chat.......

"In every typed word, a heartbeat hid — love blooming
between the lines."

"Time passed in messages so fine,

Stories shared, hearts aligned.

Each other's tales, now intertwined,

Love's journey, side by side defined."

"SanRul"

……..Our first call

"Stupidity is texting me all day, then asking, 'What's your number?'"

……………

"Picked up the phone, conversation flowed,

She Said busy, later we'll go.

'Promise(Pkka)' heard, heart felt light,

Excitement grew, for that night."

…..The Doctneer 🖤

"Medical student, dreams of healing hands,

Engineer, tech magic in demand.

Both on their own paths so bright,

Love brought them together, a perfect sight."

………………………..

"Different paths, same heart's beat,

Medical dreams, engineering feat.

Love bridged gaps, souls now align,

Together forever, hearts entwine."

..........Fix schedule

"Bank job, daily call a ritual true,

Lunch break sync, love shone through.

Fixed time talks, hearts connected deep,

Love's sweet moments, memories keep."

"SanRul"

"Complaints and displeasure too,

Didn't know it would go on so true.

But love prevailed, hearts now align,

Words from heart, now freely shine."

Wednesday, 14 June 2017

"SanRul"

"A 2 minute meeting at the station,

Helping each other with luggage in hand.

We met for a brief moment,

Conversations flowed, memories formed".

"HarSanHitaDeep"
......Love for life

.........."Stubborn in Love" 

He won't say much, but he'll never leave,

Love in his silence, hard to believe.

He hides his heart behind a frown,

Yet holds me close when I fall down.

He argues just to hear my voice,

Calls it fate, but love is his choice.

Stubborn hands, but softest touch —

He doesn't say "I love you" much...

But oh, when he does — it stays, it stays,

Like moonlight clinging to broken days.

Wednesday, 14 June 2017

"HarSanHitaDeep"
......Love for life

"SanRul"

"His stubborn nature, my silence too,

Both hurt hearts, in ways anew.

Unspoken words, issues grew wide,

Love's path challenged, hearts divide."

....

"Stubborn hearts, unspoken pain,

Both suffered, love's strain.

Words unheard, emotions high,

Love's test, hearts wondered why."

"He crossed the night, not just miles

— just to hold me for a while."

"He fought distance, bridged the gap,

Traveled far, to hear a loving tap.

But my prickly heart, a fortress high,

Kept him at bay, with a guarded sigh."

....

"He journeyed far, with love's pure fire,

But my sharp words, his heart would tire.

Torn between love and pride's dark side,

Our bond wavered, in a troubled tide."

"SanRul"

"Slowly trust grew, hearts aligned,

Love's flame kindled, souls entwined.

Doubts faded, fears lost their might,

In his eyes, my heart took flight."

....

"That moment, when hearts aligned true,

I chose to trust, and love shone through.

In his eyes, my soul found a home,

Together we stood, no longer alone."

Chapter 2:

"Coffee, Chaos & Chemistry"

"SanRul"

— And our story finally began." 

"Our first meet, at FKC Cafe's nest,

Hot and cold coffee, our love's quest.

In each other's eyes, hearts took flight,

A spark ignited, on that fateful night."

....

"Our first meet, at Fkc Cafe's place,

You in yellow tee, I in red embrace.

Hot and cold coffee, our flavors blend,

Our hearts collided, a love trend."

"After that, Akshay Patra Temple's divine,

I held his hand, and love did shine.

Inside, prayers whispered, hearts now one,

He felt my love, our bond had just begun."

....

"Every prayer I whisper is with you, and for you —even when you're silent, even when you're far." 🙏 🖤

"Two hearts, one scooty

A memorable ride 🖤

"Scooty ride, wind in our hair,

Dropped you off, with a tender air.

'Get off now,' I said with a smile so bright,

Our moments together, a precious night."

"Next day's surprise, at JC's place,

A sudden hug, love's warm embrace.

Unspoken bond, hearts now aligned,

A moment's magic, love's sweet design."

....

"In JC's vibrant space, we met again,

A hug so sudden, love's sweet refrain.

Perhaps in that touch, our hearts did say,

'I'm yours, you're mine, in every way'."

Tu Muje Ese Q Dekh Rha Hai..??

"Hours spent, gazing at me so fine, loving me dear, yet anger's constant sign."

"Watching me, with love so true, yet anger's spark, a question or two."

"Gazing eyes, a loving stare, anger's flash, a question to share."

"SanRul"

"As I leave, memories we made,

Pieces of heart, with you I've laid.

In every step, your love I'll bear,

Forever with me, our moments we'll share."

....

"I'm taking memories, laughter and tears,

Moments we shared, through all the years.

Your love, your smile, forever in mind,

A piece of my heart, I'll leave behind."

"SanRul"

"As he departed, words unspoken deep,

'Parul, i'm taking much with me,' he'd keep.

His eyes spoke volumes, heart's silent tale,

Love's imprint, forever to prevail."

....

"As I depart, your love I hold tight,

In my heart, memories of our night.

Though I'm leaving, you're not far,

In my thoughts, our love shines like a star."

Chapter 3:

Conversations On Alr.

"SanRul"

"As time passed, we grew to know each other more,

Conversations flowed, and hearts opened wide.

Though words were few, our eyes spoke volumes true,

Feelings for each other, forever shining through".

"HarSanHitaDeep"
......Love for life

"SanRul"

"As I step away, your love remains,

In my soul, our moments sustain.

Though distance grows, you're always near,

In my dreams, our love forever clear."

"HarSanHitaDeep"
......Love for life

" SanRul"

"I always talk, you always hear,

My complaint is, why don't you speak dear?

You say I'm always talking, won't let you share,

But in my heart, our love is beyond compare".

Chapter 4:

The Day My World Shifted.

"SanRul"

"A garden meeting, on a bench so fine,

You asked for a kiss, and sealed it divine.

On my forehead, your lips did stray,

In that moment, our love found its way.

Hands in hands, we'd meet for long,

Resting my head, on your shoulder strong".

"HarSanHitaDeep"
......Love for life

"SanRul"

"Hands in hands, we'd meet for hours so bright,

Resting my head, on your shoulder so tight.

In your eyes, my heart finds its nest,

With you, my love, I am forever blessed.

Your sadness, when we parted ways,

Was a sight, I'd cherish all my days".

"SanRul"

"My every pout, you'd patiently bear,

Hours of effort, to show me you care.

I loved not the fight, but your gentle way,

To bring a smile, and chase my blues away".

"HarSanHitaDeep"
......Love for life

Part II:

"Through the Storm"

&

Love – But Stronger

Fights That Left Us Speechless.......

"My blocks and silence, your every attempt,

To reach out to me, with love that's bent.

Fear of losing you, was always near,

In your eyes, my heart would fear".

"SanRul"

"The long fights, and your gentle stride,

Coming to meet me, with love inside.

One meeting with you, and my anger fades,

In your presence, my heart is gently made".

Wednesday, 14 June 2017

" I admit, you loved me more deeply,

But does that prove, I loved you not at all?

My love may have differed, in its own way,

Yet, in my heart, our moments still stay."

"SanRul"

Your constant fights, to meet me every day,

My constant refusals, in a stubborn way.

Yet, you'd still come, and I'd miss my class,

Our love was strong, but priorities would clash.

"SanRul"

Years went by, in fights and disagreements too,

But our loyalty, remained forever true.

Through thick and thin, we stood as one,

Our bond grew stronger, the trials we'd been through.

"HarSanHitaDeep"
......Love for life

"SanRul"

Meeting you made me realize,

Lust isn't everything, love's in the eyes.

In your presence, my heart finds peace,

Love's not just desire, but a gentle release.

"HarSanHitaDeep"
......Love for life

"SanRul"

"HarSanHitaDeep"

Meeting you, I realized love's true face,

Desire's not the only thing in a warm embrace.

Your eyes, a peaceful haven for my soul,

Love's a gentle touch, making my heart whole.

"Your every pout, I'd wait to see,

Hours of yours, just to make me happy.

Not just your anger, but your smile too,

Making you happy, was my heart's cue."

"SanRul"

— An engineer helping his doctor love! 

"An engineer among med students so fine,

Creating assignments that truly shine."

"Engineer in med school, a rare sight,

Crafting assignments with all their might."

"SanRul"

"My exams, his tension too,

Supporting me through, that's what he'd do."

"My stress, his concern so true,

Helping me through, exams anew."

An engineer helping with med study anew."

True love is when, my exams are his worry,

An engineer guiding me, in medical study merry

"

"Sitting together, hand in hand,

in nature's lap so grand."

"Your shoulder's gentle slope,

a resting place for my hope."

"In the garden's peaceful hue,

our hearts find solace anew.

"

"SanRul"

"

"Your love shines bright,

like a guiding light."

"In your eyes, my heart finds its home."

"With you, my soul feels complete, never alone."

"Your touch ignites,

a burning fire so bright."

"With every breath, I'll love you till the end of time.

"

"SanRul"

"Your visits to my college place,

waiting hours for my face."

"Showing me your playful ways,

still loving me through all my days."

"In your patience, I find my peace,

with you, my heart releases."

"Your love for me, a constant theme,

through laughter and life's scheme."

"His first Valentine felt less like a date...
more like an exam he didn't study for — but
hoped to pass with love."

"Our first Valentine's Week, a surprise to seek,
Doraemon and cup, gifts unique."

"You know I don't love Valentine's cheer, yet your gifts
brought joy near."

"In Doraemon's smile, I see your care, the cup, a symbol
of love we share."

"Bunked college, but learned everything about love — from your eyes, not textbooks."

"Skipping college, exams too,

for love that's true."

"Bunking classes, just to be,

with you, my love, wild and free."

"In your eyes, my heart finds a place,

skipping exams, a loving space."

....

"Skipping books, for love's sweet looks."

"Classes fade, when love's displayed."

"In your love, I find my degree."

"SanRul"

"Praying at every temple, for you to be mine,

Always by your side, my heart entwines."

"In every prayer, I wish for you,

To be with you, my love, forever true."

"Temples and prayers, a love so divine,

With you, my heart, forever aligned."

"Imperfect souls, tangled hearts — yet somehow, perfect together."

"Love's perfection, in your heart's affection."

"With you, my love, my heart finds perfection."

"In your eyes, love's true affection."

......Love for life

"The pink city blushed

"In Jaipur's streets, with you I'd meet,

Temples and gardens, our love's sweet retreat."

"With you, Jaipur's beauty shines,

In every place, our love entwines."

"Temples and gardens, a romantic place,

With you, my love, a perfect pace."

"SanRul"

"Late night rides, with you by my side,

Scolding at home, but love won't subside."

"Scooter's thrill, under starry skies,

With you, my love, our hearts' sweet surprise."

"Amer's charm, in the evening light,

With you, my love, everything's just right."

"SanRul"

"Fighting for love, in every glance,

Your patience, our relationship's second chance."

"Refusing words, but love's in every fight,

Your patience, our love's guiding light."

"In every fight, a love so true, your patience,

My heart beats for you."

"SanRul"

"In every fight, a love so bright,

your patience guides us through the night."

"With every refusal, our love grows strong,

your patience keeps us moving along."

"Fighting for love, with hearts so true,

your patience is what sees us through."

"You engineer, my med papers write,

Tense about my exams, day and night."

"Wishes and care, in every line,

Your support, my heart entwines."

"Your anger's spark, when I don't reply,

Shows how much you care, and I feel alive."

"SanRul"

"Ganesh Ji's blessings, in every care,

your love, my heart's repair."

"Small details matter, in every deed,

your love, my success' creed."

"Presentations shine, with your design,

your love, my heart's rhyme."

"SanRul"

"Gifts and surprises, on special days,

your love, in every thoughtful way."

"Remote car's joy, a child's delight,

your love, shining with all your might."

"Anger fades, with gifts so fine,

your love, forever on my mind."

"SanRul"

"Chosen and loved, my heart's delight,

With you, my love, everything's just right."

"In your eyes, my love's proof I see,

With you, my heart beats wild and free."

"Your love's my truth, my heart's my guide,

With you, my love, i'll always reside."

"SanRul"

"Old photos tell stories of our past,

Memories that forever will last."

"In every frame, a tale unfolds,

Of laughter, love, and moments told."

"Photos of us, in places we'd roam,

Chai and cafes, our love's sweet home."

Dance on 'Hawaayein'.........

"Dancing feet, hearts so light,

'Hawaayein' song, a sweet delight."

"Cute moves, love shines bright,

In every step, our hearts take flight."

"Amazing dance, you stole the show,

With every beat, our love will grow."

"SanRul"

"Private moments, just you and me,

Dancing to 'Hawaayein', wild and free."

"Cute steps, in our own space,

Love's sweetness, in every gentle pace."

"Amazing dancer, in my eyes,

Our private dance, a sweet surprise."

……Love for life

"**Promises? made**, on special days,

Cake and love, in sweet, sweet ways."

"Birthday dreams, of cake so fine,

Promises kept, love that's truly mine."

"Cake for you, a promise so true,

On your special day, my love shines through."

"SanRul"

"Love letters sweet, heart's every line,

Before we meet, love's divine."

"Ink flows free, heart's every thought,

Meeting soon, love's plot."

"Letters to me, heart's every beat,

Plans for us, love's sweet treat."

"SanRul"

"Night travels long, to meet you strong,

College waits, but love's song."

"Garden talks, hours pass by slow,

Love's whispers, heart's sweet glow."

"Slowly mine, in love's sweet pace,

Heartbeats sync, a perfect place."

"SanRul"

"Central Park's memories so bright,

Fights and love, in the morning light."

"Walking side by side, hand in hand,

Love's sweet moments, in a beautiful land."

"Fights fade away, love shines so bright,

In Central Park, our hearts take flight."

— you're my favorite flower."

"Roses given, though not my flair,

love's gesture, with a hint of care."

"You knew my likes, yet roses brought,

love's surprise, with a thoughtful thought."

"Stress and love, a complex blend,

roses for you, my heart's true friend."

"SanRul"

"Roses in hand, a loving stand,

Though not my favorite, love's thoughtful plan."

"You knew my heart,

Yet roses apart, love's gesture, a loving art."

"Stress and love, a delicate dance,

Roses for you, a romantic chance."

"Station's bitter fight, love's sweet plight,

Sulking walks, Remember that night.?

"Fighting words, at the station cold,

Love's warmth, in apologies told."

"Walked away, with a heavy heart, f

Ollowed close, a brand new start."

"SanRul"

"Years went by, in meetings sweet,

Love's next step, romance to greet."

"Talks and time, love's gentle climb,

Romance needed, heart's rhyme."

"Love's journey long, talks and more,

Romance's spark, forever in store."

"HarSanHitaDeep"
.....Love for life

"SanRul"

"Insistent meets, alone we'd stray,

Anger's spark, love's gentle way."

"Meetings solo, a stubborn plea,

Anger fades, love's romance to see."

"Alone we'd meet, a test of will,

Love's understanding, romance to fulfill."

"SanRul"

"Home for a visit, a brother's claim,

Proved me wrong, love's sweet game."

"Came home briefly, a bond to share,

Proved assumptions wrong, love to spare."

"A visit home, a brother's guise,

Love shone through, a sweet surprise."

"SanRul"

"Home again, a sweet delight,

Dew and kachoris, a lovely sight."

"Love and laughter, photos to share,

Memories made, with love to spare."

"Dew and treats, a party so fine,

Love and photos, a memory divine."

"Planning done, a trip so fine,

Nahargarh Zoo, scooty's gentle shine."

"Scooty ride, through zoo's delight,

Animals near, a wondrous sight."

"Nahargarh's charm, a visit so rare,

Scooty's thrill, animals to share."

"SanRul"

"Stressful life, a soothing nest,

Head on lap, eternal rest."

"Life's chaos, a calm retreat,

Lap's warmth, a heart that beats."

"Tired soul, a peaceful place,

Head on lap, a loving space."

"SanRul"

"Birthday's joy, at my place so dear,

Cake with KALU name, love that's clear."

"Daal bati's taste, a dinner so fine,

Night with you, a love divine."

"Special night, a celebration so rare,

Cake and dinner, love to share."

.........So Meri Rani So Meri Rani

"Lullaby's charm, a nightly song,

Sleep my queen, love so strong."

"Phone's gentle voice, a soothing tale,

Sleep my queen, love that prevails."

"Nightly serenade, a lullaby sweet,

Sleep my queen, love's gentle beat."

............**A Home for US.**

"Galta's charm, a memory so bright,

Building home, with love's delight."

"Stone's foundation, a dream so true,

Harsanhitadeep, a home for you."

"Temple's beauty, a love so rare,

Harsanhitadeep, a home to share."

"Love's unknown, he showed the way,

romance bloomed, in a crazy sway."

"Crazy love, a heart so true,

asking always, 'Just for you?'"

"Unknown love, he lit the flame,

romance grew, with love's sweet name."

.... The DoctNeer 🩶

"Love's the diagnosis, heart's the cure,

DocTNeer fixes, love that's pure."

"Heartbeat's rhythm, love's sweet sound,

DocTNeer listens, without a bound."

"No tools needed, love's the key,

DocTNeer fixes, heart's melody."

"SanRul"

"Heartbeat's pulse, love's gentle touch,

DocTNeer heals, with a loving clutch."

"Love's the prescription, heart's the cure,

DocTNeer mends, with love that's pure."

"No stethoscope, just love's keen ear,

DocTNeer listens, to heart's every fear."

"SanRul"

"Love's rollercoaster, ups and downs,

Breakups daily, yet love's renowned."

"Ten breakups a day, love's peculiar way,

Together apart, yet love stays."

"Break and make, our love's own pace,

Can't live with, can't live without the chase."

.......He In Saree

"Sarees for love, a crazy delight,

Boy's sweet gesture, shining bright."

"Crazy boy, wears sarees with glee,

Love's unique charm, for you and me."

"Love's fashion, sarees so fine,

Crazy boy's style, all the time."

"SanRul"

"2 am, roof's quiet space,

You, me, wifi, coffee's gentle pace."

"Midnight's calm, roof's peaceful nest,

Coffee's warmth, wifi's gentle quest."

"Roof's serenity, 2 am's delight,

Coffee and wifi, our quiet night."

"SanRul"

"Prayag's us place, love's sweet fate,

Romance blooms, hearts create."

"Distances fade, love's gentle stream,

Prayag's meeting, a romantic dream."

"Love's moments pure, in Prayag's embrace,

Hearts unite, a loving space."

"SanRul"

"Fun kingdom's play, wrestling's delight,

Swings of joy, childhood's sweet night."

"Wrestling fun, with you by side,

Swings and laughter, childhood's joyful ride."

"Kingdom of fun, memories so bright,

Wrestling and swings, pure delight."

"SanRul"

......Love for life

"Temple's peace, your gentle care,

Tying laces, love we share."

"Prayers for you, in temple's grace,

Siddhat of love, in every place."

"Laces tied, heart's sweet bond,

Sandeep, my love, forever beyond."

"You are Lord Shiva's blessing in my life —

"Mahakal's blessings, thread of fate,

4 years of prayer, your love to create."

"Thread tied tight, heart's pure prayer,

Mahakal's grace, you always there."

"4 years of devotion, thread's sweet tie,

Mahakal's blessing, you by my side."

Part III:

"The Family Walls"

"SanRul"

Us vs. Them...............

"Time was kind, but now it's cold,

Fights for family, love grows old."

"Once for us, now for the crowd,

Love's battle, in a different cloud."

"Family's gaze, society's might,

Our love's fight, in plain sight."

"SanRul"

"Battles within, battles loud,

No reason clear, but fights avowed."

"Fights for what, for whom, for why,

Family ties, a complicated sigh."

"Some fights are won, some lost in time,

Family expectations, a heavy chime."

"SanRul"

"Misunderstandings, in love's dark night,

Need and support, a constant fight."

"Love's meaning deep, one or two,

In every heart, a different view."

"Support and love, a complex dance,

Need and want, a delicate trance."

"A time came when we became

Enemies to each other."

When We Forgot

We Were on the Same Side"

"SanRul"

......Love for life

"Time turned cold, love grew apart,

Enemies in heart."

"Moments passed, love turned to pain,

Enemies we became, in vain."

"Once united, now we stand apart,

Enemies in heart, a broken start."

_"Harshdeep, love for lifee

"Life's beauty shines, love's pure light,

Harshdeep, you, my delight."

"Harshdeep, love's gentle stream,

Life's joy, you, my dream."

"Love for lifee, you by my side,

Harshdeep, my heart's pride."

Part IV:

The Break We Didn't Want

"SanRul"

A Chapter Left Unwritten...

Every love story has its share of sunshine and storms —
and sometimes, the silence says more than words ever
could.
There is a part missing in this book. Yes, I will write it
one day. But not today.
Because that part wasn't just ours. It involved hearts
beyond ours — families, hopes, fears, and expectations
that shaped the path we walked.

To write it, I'd have to unfold wounds that still breathe
quietly beneath the surface.
So for now, let this gap speak gently. The love was real.
So was the struggle.
And one day, when time is kinder, I'll write the rest.

Best regards,

Dr Harshita S Jaiman

Part V:

Finding My Way Back to Us

When the Universe Whispered "Try Again"

"This time we've chosen, love will prevail,

Family and norms won't prevail,our love will set sail."

"We've made up our minds, love won't be tamed,

This time it's ours, no one can claim."

"Our hearts have decided, love will win the fight,

No matter what others say, our love shines bright."

"SanRul"

"Through trials and strife, we stood as one,

Family bonds tested, but love had won."

"Fighting for love, through every test,

Family ties that bind, we did our best."

"In the fire of strife, we found our way,

Family love that shines, come what may."

"Family issues brewed, silent fights,

Unspoken words, a heavy plight."

"Words unspoken, battles raged,

Family ties strained, emotions engaged."

"Silent screams, unspoken pain,

Family conflicts, love in vain.

Love — But Stronger

"After years of strife, they finally won,

Love conquered all, the battle done."

"Through struggles and pain, we rose above,

Love's flame burning bright, a labor of love."

"Years of fight, but love shone through,

The victory sweet, a bond anew."

"SanRul"

"Both stubborn hearts, finally tied the knot,

Love's persistence, a bond they've got."

"Ziddi both, but love made them one,

Marriage bells rang, a new life begun."

"Stubborn souls, but love prevailed,

Marriage vows exchanged, hearts no longer failed."

"SanRul"

......Love for life

"From two hearts beating, to one love true,

Best friends to married couple, a journey anew."

"2010's spark, ignited a flame,

Best friends to partners, love's sweet name."

"From friendship's roots to love's sweet fruit,
Harshdeep's bond, forever to suit."

---Our Ending That Feels,

Like a New Beginning.

2010 to 11-12-2024

.

New Beginning With Old Memories……

"SanRul"

Once More......

"A delayed train, life's winding way,

A journey's pause, love's gentle sway.

We travel on, through every stage,

Life's adventure, a love filled page."

"Love's train, destination forever,

a boy and a girl's love will forever be."

"Hand in hand, love's train journey,

every stop, love's beauty."

"Love's station, waiting for you,

a boy and a girl's love forever true."

"Attention please, dear passengers--

Train number 14062017 — the love train —
has finally arrived, not on time, but right on
destiny.
It traveled through seasons and years,
crossing distances, delays, and doubts,
only to find its way to this very moment.
Two souls, long separated by life's
timetable,
now stand on the same platform —
ready to board forever, together.
Love may be late, but it never misses its
station."

@11-12-2024

Afterword: A Love That Wrote Itself

This is not the end—only a comma in the story that still breathes.

As I finish these pages, I don't feel like I've written a book. I feel like I've opened a window—into memories that once danced quietly in my mind, into moments that made my heart louder, and into a love that refused to be forgotten.

This wasn't perfect. Neither were we. But that's what made it real.

There were days when silence was louder than words. Nights when distance felt colder than miles. Fights that broke us for a moment. Forgiveness that stitched us back, slowly but surely.

We loved not like the movies, but like mornings after storms—messy, beautiful, and full of hope.

If you're holding this book, you're holding proof that even with flaws, misunderstandings, time,

and chaos—love survives. It may change shape. It may pause. But it doesn't die if it's real.

And maybe this is the bravest thing I've done: not loving you—but telling the world how deeply I did.

To the one who inspired of this: You were never just a chapter. You were the ink. And no matter how far life carries us… You will always be my favourite sentence.

Yes Its you My favourite Person, my love, my best friend, and of course now my husband too. (_Sandeep Guru.)

_Dr Harshita S Jaiman

About the Author

The Heart Behind These Pages

Dr. Harshita S. Jaiman

A dreamer in a white coat, **Dr. Harshita S. Jaiman** balances the precision of medicine with the chaos of emotions. Between clinical rounds and quiet reflections, she found herself drawn to stories—especially the one her heart lived.

This is not just a book. It's a whisper of her truth, a tribute to moments that shaped her, and a gentle reminder that even the busiest hearts can still ache, hope, and love deeply.

Through these pages, she doesn't claim to be a writer—only someone who couldn't stay silent about what love once felt like.

ATTENTION PLEASE

140617 — the love train — has
finally arrived, not on time,
but right on destiny
It traveled through
seasons and years,
crossing distances,
delays, and doubts,
only to find its way
to this very
moment.
Two souls, long
separated by life's
timetable, now
stand on the same
platform — ready to board
forever, together.

140617 wasn't punctual, but
it always traveled toward each
ether.*

www.ingramcontent.com/pod-product-compliance
Lightning Source LLC
Chambersburg PA
CBHW041332120726
48005CB00014B/2216